PENGUIN YOUNG READERS

LEVEL 3
TRANSITIONAL READER

Baby Otter

D0017787

by Ginjer L. Clarke
illustrated by Robbin Cuddy

Penguin Young Readers
An Imprint of Penguin Group (USA) Inc.

Whoosh! What was that?

A river otter popped out of the water. It climbed up into a tunnel under some tree roots. River otters are fast and shy. They mostly come out at night.

Dear Parents and Educators,

Welcome to Penguin Young Readers! As parents and educators, you know that each child develops at his or her own pace—in terms of speech, critical thinking, and, of course, reading. Penguin Young Readers recognizes this fact. As a result, each Penguin Young Readers book is assigned a traditional easy-to-read level (1–4) as well as a Guided Reading Level (A–P). Both of these systems will help you choose the right book for your child. Please refer to the back of each book for specific leveling information. Penguin Young Readers features esteemed authors and illustrators, stories about favorite characters, fascinating nonfiction, and more!

Baby Otter

LEVEL **3**

GUIDED READING LEVEL **M**

This book is perfect for a **Transitional Reader** who:
- can read multisyllable and compound words;
- can read words with prefixes and suffixes;
- is able to identify story elements (beginning, middle, end, plot, setting, characters, problem, solution); and
- can understand different points of view.

Here are some **activities** you can do during and after reading this book:
- Nonfiction: Nonfiction books deal with facts and events that are real. Talk about the elements of nonfiction. On a separate sheet of paper, write down the facts you learned about baby otters. Then write down the facts you learned about adult otters.
- Comprehension: Answer the following questions about otters.
  - How do baby otters play?
  - What animals are dangerous to baby otters?
  - Why do otters close up the openings to tunnels in the riverbanks during the wintertime?
  - How deep can sea otters dive?

Remember, sharing the love of reading with a child is the best gift you can give!

—Bonnie Bader, EdM
  Penguin Young Readers program

*Penguin Young Readers are leveled by independent reviewers applying the standards developed by Irene Fountas and Gay Su Pinnell in *Matching Books to Readers: Using Leveled Books in Guided Reading*, Heinemann, 1999.

To moms everywhere,
both human and animal, for taking on
the hardest job in the world—GLC

For my aunt Lorraine,
who is a bright light in this world—RC

Penguin Young Readers
Published by the Penguin Group
Penguin Group (USA) Inc., 375 Hudson Street, New York, New York 10014, USA
Penguin Group (Canada), 90 Eglinton Avenue East, Suite 700, Toronto, Ontario M4P 2Y3, Canada
(a division of Pearson Penguin Canada Inc.)
Penguin Books Ltd, 80 Strand, London WC2R 0RL, England
Penguin Ireland, 25 St Stephen's Green, Dublin 2, Ireland (a division of Penguin Books Ltd)
Penguin Group (Australia), 707 Collins Street, Melbourne, Victoria 3008, Australia
(a division of Pearson Australia Group Pty Ltd)
Penguin Books India Pvt Ltd, 11 Community Centre, Panchsheel Park, New Delhi—110 017, India
Penguin Group (NZ), 67 Apollo Drive, Rosedale, Auckland 0632, New Zealand
(a division of Pearson New Zealand Ltd)
Penguin Books, Rosebank Office Park, 181 Jan Smuts Avenue, Parktown North 2193, South Africa
Penguin China, B7 Jaiming Center, 27 East Third Ring Road North,
Chaoyang District, Beijing 100020, China

Penguin Books Ltd, Registered Offices: 80 Strand, London WC2R 0RL, England

All rights reserved. No part of this book may be reproduced, scanned, or distributed in any printed or
electronic form without permission. Please do not participate in or encourage piracy of copyrighted
materials in violation of the author's rights. Purchase only authorized editions.

Text copyright © 2009 by Ginjer L. Clarke. Illustrations copyright © 2009 by Robbin Cuddy. All rights
reserved. First published in 2009 by Grosset & Dunlap, an imprint of Penguin Group (USA) Inc.
Published in 2013 by Penguin Young Readers, an imprint of Penguin Group (USA) Inc.,
345 Hudson Street, New York, New York 10014. Manufactured in China.

Library of Congress Control Number: 2009015706

ISBN 978-0-448-45105-3   10 9 8 7 6 5 4 3 2

ALWAYS LEARNING   PEARSON

North American river otters live in the United States and Canada. They make their homes near marshes, rivers, and streams. Otters use dens made by beavers or other animals who have moved out.

This female otter crawls through a tight tunnel into her roomy den. The den is dark, so she can sleep during the daytime.

She has lined the den with dry
leaves to make it cozy during the
cold winter. Now that it is almost
spring, she is about to have babies!

The mother otter has given birth to three tiny otter cubs. They are hairless, blind, and only about four inches long. You could fit one in your hand!

Their mother cuddles them to
keep them warm. They will drink
only their mother's milk for now.
But mostly they sleep a lot. Sweet
dreams, baby otters.

As the baby otters grow, they play
with their mother and with one
another. River otters play more than
most wild animals. Otter cubs love to
wrestle!

They tumble and roll around their
den. They climb and crawl all over
their mother. She swats them gently
if they get too rough.

A few times a week, the mother otter leaves the den to get food for herself. She does not go far. She squeaks loudly to tell her cubs that she is nearby.

The cubs are curious about what is outside of the den. They peek out the hole at the end of the tunnel to see the sky and the river. They sniff the air outside, but they do not leave yet.

Two months have passed since the baby otters were born. Now it is springtime. The cubs are twice as big. They can see and hear. And they have short, black fur.

The mother otter leads her cubs out of the den. Everything the baby otters see is strange and new to them. They are afraid to leave home. Their mother chirps softly to tell them they are safe.

The baby otters follow their
mother onto the riverbank. They
wobble on their short legs until they
get used to walking. Soon they are
off and running!

The otter cubs like to explore, but they are also hungry. They find insects and worms for their first big meal. The cubs will have to learn to swim before they can catch fish.

It is time for swim lessons.

Zip! The mother otter slides down the bank to show her cubs how to get into the water. She is so sleek that she barely makes a ripple when she dives into the water.

Otters are great swimmers. But the baby otters do not know this yet. They are afraid of the swirling, cold water. They huddle on the bank and watch their mother.

The mother otter calls to her cubs
to come in. But they do not move.
She climbs back up the bank and
pushes them with her nose.

20

Splash! One cub falls into the river. The next one slides in the mud. The last cub still will not go. The mother pushes it gently into the water. The baby otters are swimming!

Otters are made for the water.
They close their ears and nose to
keep the water out. They steer with
their long tails and paddle with their
back feet. Their thick fur keeps them
warm.

At first, the baby otters float and follow their mother. The shy otter cub rides on his mother's back. They are getting used to being in the water today.

Uh-oh! The mother otter sees a coyote watching her babies from across the river. Coyotes, bobcats, foxes, large birds, and alligators will hurt baby otters if the babies are left alone.

The mother otter whistles to tell her babies that danger is near. The otter family swims quickly back to the tunnel. They scamper inside their den, where they will be safe.

Back inside the den, the mother otter shows the cubs how to clean their fur. River otters have thick fur that is waterproof and keeps their skin dry and warm.

The baby otters use their webbed
front paws to comb through their
fur. Then the otter family rests. The
cubs have had a big first day outside.

The next day, the otters practice swimming again. After a few more days, the cubs are ready to dive. Their mother tosses a shell in the air with her nose. It falls into the water.

The cubs dive down to the river bottom to get the shell.

Zoom! They twist and twirl under the water. They swim upside down and flip all around. Otters love to play!

While they are still babies, the cubs eat food that their mother catches for them. They eat frogs, turtles, snakes, clams, crayfish, small birds, and lots of fish.

Today, the mother otter finds their favorite snack—a crayfish.

Crunch! She cracks open the crayfish and lets her cubs have a few small bites. Then they clean their faces and whiskers in the grass.

A few months later, the baby otters try hunting on their own. One of the otter cubs swims to the bottom of the river. She uses her whiskers to feel for food in the muddy water.

Snap! A crab tries to pinch the otter when she comes close. The baby otter is surprised. The crab moves away fast. Better luck next time!

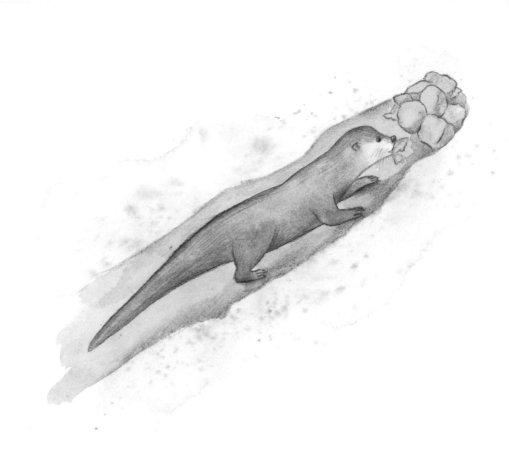

All summer, the otter cubs learned to swim and find food. Now it is wintertime again. The cubs help their mother close up the opening to the tunnel in the riverbank. This keeps their den warm.

They use their front claws to dig
another tunnel that comes out below
water. They need to find food after
the river is covered in ice. Otters
swim under the ice. They can hold
their breath for up to eight minutes!

When spring comes again, the otter cubs are grown up. They are three to four feet long and weigh up to 30 pounds. That is about the size of a small dog, with a very long tail.

Their black fur has turned dark reddish brown all over and silver on their faces and chests. It is time for them to leave home. They are ready to find mates. And their mother is ready to have more babies.

River otters are becoming rare in many places. Humans are their only threat. Otters are hunted for their fur, but that is illegal in many places.

River otters are running out of
space to live and swim in. Forests are
being cut down, and rivers are being
polluted. You can help keep rivers
clean. We want river otters to have
a place to live for a long time!

Many zoos and aquariums keep
river otters in large tanks, so you
can watch them playing. This helps
people learn more about these
animals and gives injured otters
a place to live.

Pairs of otters play together and show that they love each other. They roll and cuddle in the water. Sometimes they give each other gentle love bites on the neck.

Silly river otters!

North American river otters have cousins all over the world. European otters look the same, but live in Europe and Asia. Their favorite food is slippery European eels. *Yuck!*

African clawless otters live mostly in south and central Africa. Their paws look like fingers because they do not have claws. An African otter can catch an octopus in its mouth and crush it with its large, sharp teeth.

Giant otters live only in the rain forests of South America. They grow up to six feet long—twice as big as river otters. They have wide, flat tails to help them swim very fast.

Unlike other river otters, giant otters live in groups. The parents, baby otters, and younger adults all stay together in one den. They are one big, happy family.

Sea otters spend almost all of their lives in the ocean. They eat, sleep, and play together in very large groups. Sea otters can dive as much as 100 feet down to find food!

This mother sea otter floats on a bed of kelp. When she eats, she uses her belly like a dinner table. She holds her new baby on her tummy while they rest. What a comfy way to sleep!

All otters love to play. They twirl underwater, slip in the mud, and slide in the snow.

Do you like to have fun like a baby otter?